TELESCOPES

© Aladdin Books Ltd 1991

*First published in
the United States in 1991 by*
Gloucester Press
387 Park Avenue South
New York NY 10016

Design David West
Children's Book Design

Editorial Lionheart Books

Consultant Robert Forrest, Hatfield Polytechnic, England

Picture Research Emma Krikler

Illustrator Ian Moores

Printed in Belgium

Library of Congress Cataloging-in-Publication Data

Bender, Lionel.
    Telescopes / Lionel Bender.
       p.   cm. -- (How it works)
    Includes index.
    Summary: Demonstrates how telescopes operate,
from the simplest to the most complex and
sophisticated.
    ISBN 0-531-17265-1
    1. Telescopes--Juvenile literature. [1. Telescopes.]
I. Title. II. Series.
QB88.B46   1991
522'.2--dc20   91-7802   CIP   AC

The publishers wish to point out that all the
photographs reproduced in this book have been either
posed by models or obtained from photographic
agencies.

CONTENTS

HOW · IT · WORKS

TELESCOPES

LIONEL BENDER

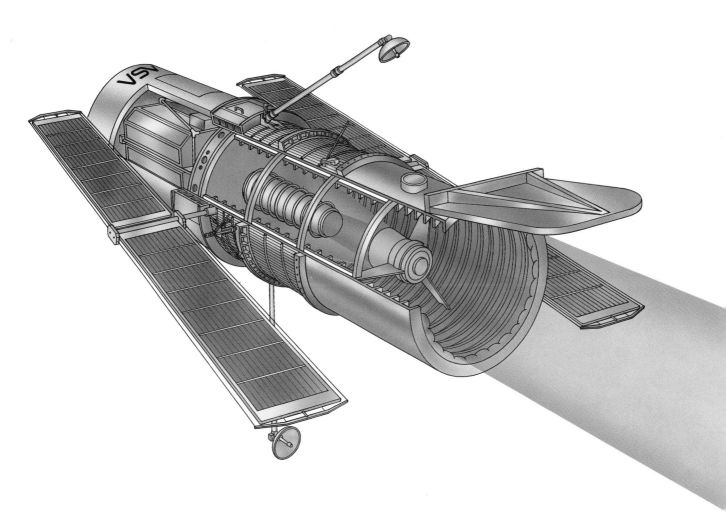

GLOUCESTER PRESS

New York · London · Toronto · Sydney

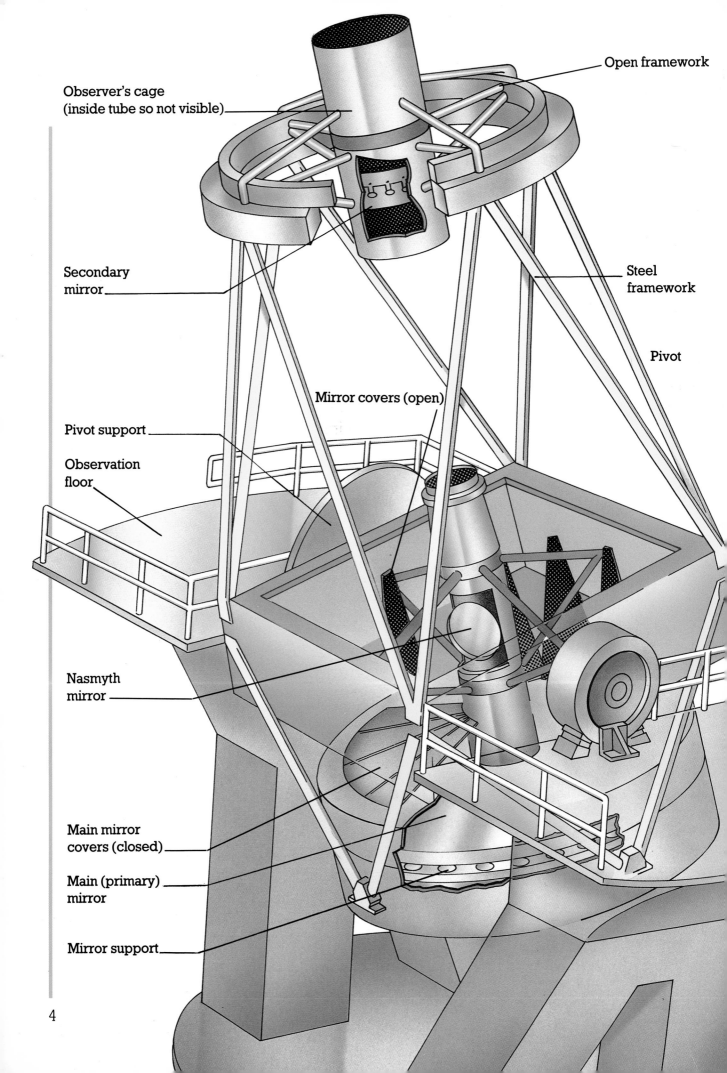

Open framework

Observer's cage
(inside tube so not visible)

Secondary
mirror

Steel
framework

Pivot

Pivot support

Mirror covers (open)

Observation
floor

Nasmyth
mirror

Main mirror
covers (closed)

Main (primary)
mirror

Mirror support

THE WORKING PARTS

On a clear night, away from the glare of city lights, it is possible to see thousands of stars in the sky. There are in fact hundreds of thousands of stars visible in the night sky, but most of them are too dim to be seen with the naked eye. Many of these can be seen by using binoculars or a telescope. The other planets in our star system, the Solar System, can also be studied in greater detail with binoculars or a telescope.

The telescope shown here is a reconstructed cutaway of an instrument used by professional astronomers to study the stars and planets. It is known as a "reflector" because it uses mirrors to collect and direct light by reflection.

Light rays enter the telescope through the open framework at the top. They travel down to the bottom of the structure where they are reflected upward by the main, or "primary," mirror. The curved main mirror also directs the light rays so that they will come together to form a sharply focused image.

The light rays then continue up to the top of the telescope where the image becomes visible. An astronomer can sit in a cage at the top to see the image. More commonly, the light rays forming the image are directed down again by a secondary mirror and then reflected out to the side of the telescope by an angled "Nasmyth" mirror onto an observation floor. Here, astronomers have more room to analyze the image with their instruments.

The main mirror is the telescope's most important and most expensive part. Its surface is protected by a safety cover when it is not in use.

The telescope is supported by a massive base to minimize unwanted vibrations that would otherwise make the image shake. The base, also called the telescope "mount," is constructed so that the telescope can be moved by electric motors to track or follow the stars. This is necessary to keep a star or a group of stars in view as the earth spins beneath them. The telescope is protected from the weather by a dome-shaped building (not shown) with a slot-shaped opening across the top. The dome rotates until the opening is above the telescope. Doors on the slot are then opened and observing can begin.

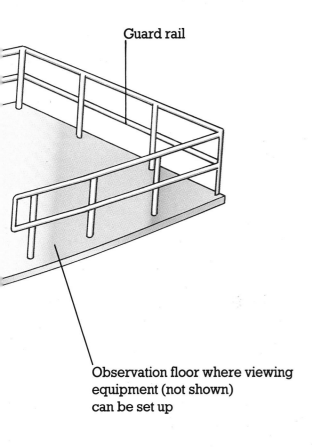

Guard rail

Observation floor where viewing equipment (not shown) can be set up

DIFFERENT TYPES

Every telescope is designed to do a particular job. Its size, shape and even where it is located are all influenced by the type and amount of *radiation* that the telescope is designed to receive. Stars send out much more radiation than the light that our eyes see. Special telescopes can detect this radiation and convert it into a form that we can see. These invisible radiations include infrared, ultraviolet, X rays and gamma rays. There are four main types of telescope:

reflectors, refractors, radio and infrared.

Most telescopes have dish-shaped, or concave, reflectors to concentrate the energy of the light or other radiation received over the whole dish onto a small, sensitive detector positioned at the point where all the radiation comes together. This is called the "prime focus" area. In an optical telescope, the "detector" could be the astronomer's eye or a camera, but today it is more likely to be an electronic sensor such

Infrared (IR) telescopes like this one work best in space as our atmosphere absorbs IR radiation.

as a photomultiplier, which makes images brighter. A radio telescope's detector is a radio receiver. Radio telescopes are often dish-shaped, but they may also be built in the form of a flat network of wires. The most powerful optical telescopes are built on top of mountains or launched into space to avoid the damaging effects of the earth's atmosphere on their images (see pages 16 and 17).

An automatic lens, or refracting, telescope.

Telescope detecting radio signals from space.

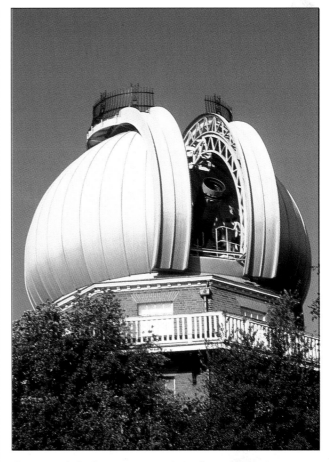

Greenwich Observatory's refracting telescope.

An amateur astronomer's reflector telescope.

Telescopes range in scale from the small, portable optical instruments used at home by amateur astronomers (above) to the vast optical and radio telescopes weighing hundreds of tons. These are housed in specially built observatories that are used by professional astronomers (top and left).

MIRRORS AND LENSES

Optical telescopes collect and focus light by using lenses or mirrors. Bending light rays with a lens is called refraction, and so telescopes that use lenses are called refractors. In all but the cheapest of models with plastic components, the lenses are made of glass. Bouncing light off a mirror is known as reflection. Telescopes that use mirrors instead of lenses are called reflectors.

If a telescope can collect more light, it can detect fainter and more distant objects. Larger lenses and mirrors collect much more light than smaller ones. However, it is difficult to make large lenses. They can only be supported around their thin rim and the weight of the lens causes it to sag, distorting the images it produces. Large mirrors are easier to make because they can be supported over their entire back surface. That is why the largest optical telescopes in the world today are all reflectors.

Scientists have devised several different ways of viewing the image produced by a reflector. The first practical one was the Newtonian developed by Sir Isaac Newton (right) in 1672. It uses a small flat mirror to reflect light out through an eyepiece in the side of the telescope. The next, named after the 17th century French astronomer Cassegrain, uses a small second mirror to reflect the light out through a central hole in the main mirror for easier viewing. In the Nasmyth type (far right), the light path is folded back on itself by one small mirror before it is brought out by another mirror through an eyepiece lens in the side of the telescope.

Refracting and reflecting
In a refractor, light rays from a distant object enter at one end, pass through a lens or several lenses, and the image is seen at the other end. In a reflector, the light path is folded back on itself by the main mirror. However, the image is focused in the path of the incoming light, where it is difficult to look at it. The problem is often solved by reflecting the image out to the side of the telescope by means of a small second mirror.

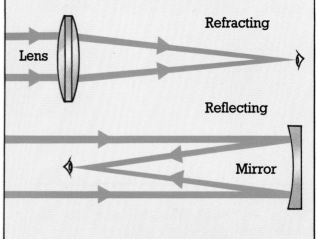

Refracting

Lens

Reflecting

Mirror

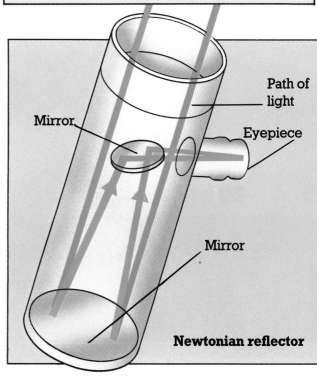

Path of light

Mirror

Eyepiece

Mirror

Newtonian reflector

8

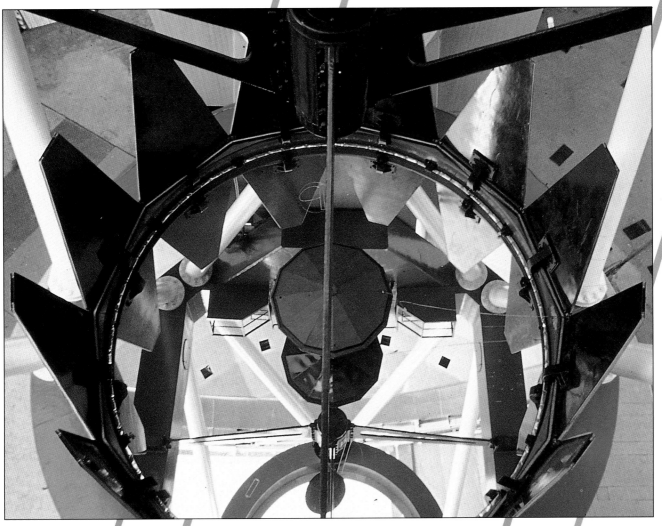

The 20-feet wide mirror inside the world's largest reflector telescope at Mt Semirodriki, USSR.

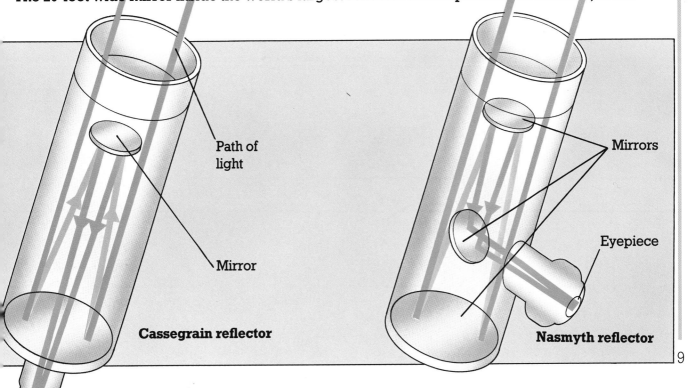

Path of
light

Mirror

Mirrors

Eyepiece

Cassegrain reflector

Nasmyth reflector

FIELD OF VIEW

Whatever can be seen through a telescope is called its field of view. A more powerful telescope – one that seems to magnify, or increase, the size of an object the most – has a *smaller* field of view than a less powerful one.

Astronomers find their way around the sky by knowing the patterns of the stars. If only a few stars are visible in the field of view, it may be difficult to recognize any patterns and find the particular object that the astronomer is looking for. For this reason, such telescopes are fitted with a finder computer or a small wide-angle telescope called a "finder telescope." This is used to locate the general area of interest. When the object that the astronomer wants to find is positioned in the middle of this field of view, it can also be seen in the middle of the high-power telescope's smaller field of view.

Only one type of telescope, called a Schmidt telescope, can produce a detailed image of a large area. It is usually called a Schmidt camera because the first Schmidt instruments could only record their images on film.

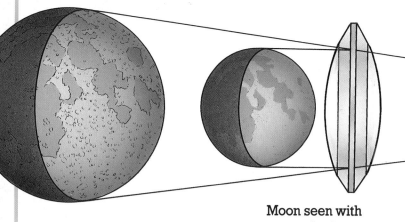

MAGNIFICATION WITH A LENS

Moon seen with naked eye

Moon seen through telescope

A convex (bulging outward) lens magnifies a distant object by bending, or refracting, the light rays traveling from it to the observer's eye. The refracted rays appear to come from a larger object.

The Schmidt camera (right) was specially designed in 1930 by Bernhard Schmidt to photograph a sharp image of a large field of view in a single image. It collects light using a 6-feet diameter mirror, but it also has a specially shaped lens to correct distortions in the image caused by the shape of the mirror. The lens is 4 feet across.

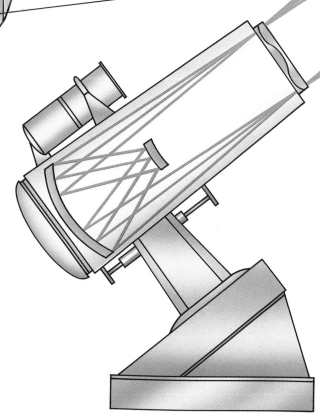

Astronomers constantly hunt for interesting objects in the sky to study. If they were to only use a high-power telescope with a tiny field of view (small circle in diagram), it would take a very long time. So first they search through a photograph taken by a wide-angle telescope such as a Schmidt (outer area). If any interesting objects or areas show up on the Schmidt image, they can be checked further with a more powerful telescope. For instance, in the cluster of stars called the Pleiades, or "Seven Sisters," a Schmidt camera can record 150 main stars and 20,000 background stars as opposed to seven seen by the naked eye or one or two with a high-powered telescope.

11

MOUNTING THE TELESCOPE

A telescope or a pair of binoculars that magnify objects by more than about seven times should be clamped to a firm support called a mounting, or mount, to hold it steady. Without a mount, if an instrument of this power is held in the hands, its image shakes too much to be clearly visible. (For similar reasons a professional photographer usually clamps his or her camera to a tripod.)

The mounting must be able to swivel so that the instrument can be turned to observe any point in the sky. A simple support called an altitude-azimuth, or altazimuth mount, allows a telescope or a pair of binoculars to be swiveled up and down and also from side to side. However, the altazimuth mount is at a serious disadvantage if a star has to be kept steadily in view for long periods, perhaps while it is being photographed. A telescope on an altazimuth mount has to be moved from time to time in both directions because the stars seem to move across the sky as the earth spins around in space.

One answer to this problem of movement is to tilt one of the supports so that it is parallel with a line through the earth's north and south poles. This type is called an equatorial mount. When a telescope supported by an equatorial mount is pointed at a star, it has to be moved in only one direction to counter the motion of the earth. A small clockwork or electric motor can be fitted to the mounting to drive it at precisely the right speed to keep the field of view steady.

A horseshoe-shaped equatorial mounting

Some types of equatorial mountings
In the fork mount (right), the telescope – colored blue – swivels between the jaws of a fork – colored purple – which itself can rotate in the base. The yoke mounting (middle right), is similar to the fork mount except that the telescope is supported on both sides. In the cross-axis mounting (far right), the weight of the telescope on one side of its cross-shaped support is balanced by a counterweight on the other side.

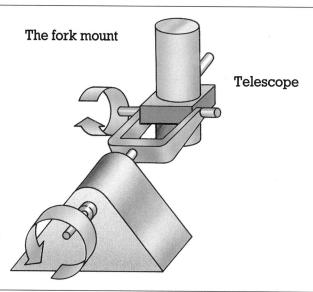

The fork mount

Telescope

The dark horsehead nebula photographed using a telescope on an equatorial mounting

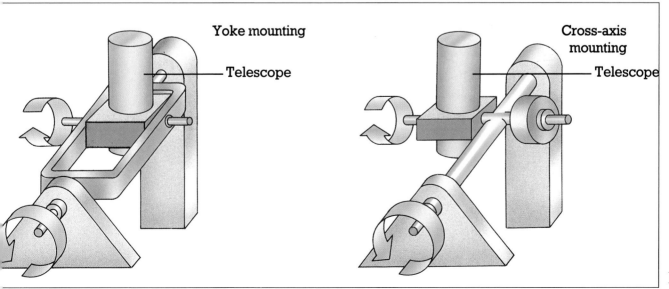

Yoke mounting

Telescope

Cross-axis mounting

Telescope

ON LAND

Astronomical telescopes create images which are upside down. This does not matter, especially in astronomy, but it is a serious disadvantage when using astronomical telescopes for bird-watching, surveying or watching sports.

Telescopes intended to be used for non-astronomical purposes are often known as terrestrial telescopes, or field telescopes. They have an extra lens or lenses, called erecting lenses or prisms, that turn the image the right-side up. The telescope is made from two or more tubes that slide inside each other. The image is brought into sharp focus by sliding the tubes to bring the lenses closer to each other or farther apart. This arrangement has given us the adjective "telescopic," which can be applied to anything that extends in the same way even if it is not a telescope, a telescopic radio aerial for example.

The field telescope has two major drawbacks. The user has to look through it with one eye while keeping the other eye closed. This can quickly become uncomfortable. Secondly, it can be quite long and therefore awkward to use in confined spaces.

Both problems are readily solved by folding the telescope up into a shorter length and putting two of them together so that the user can keep both eyes open. The result is a pair of binoculars. They are as powerful as a pair of much larger telescopes but, being compact, the binoculars are much more convenient to use.

Binoculars provide the most convenient way of getting good close-up views of wildlife.

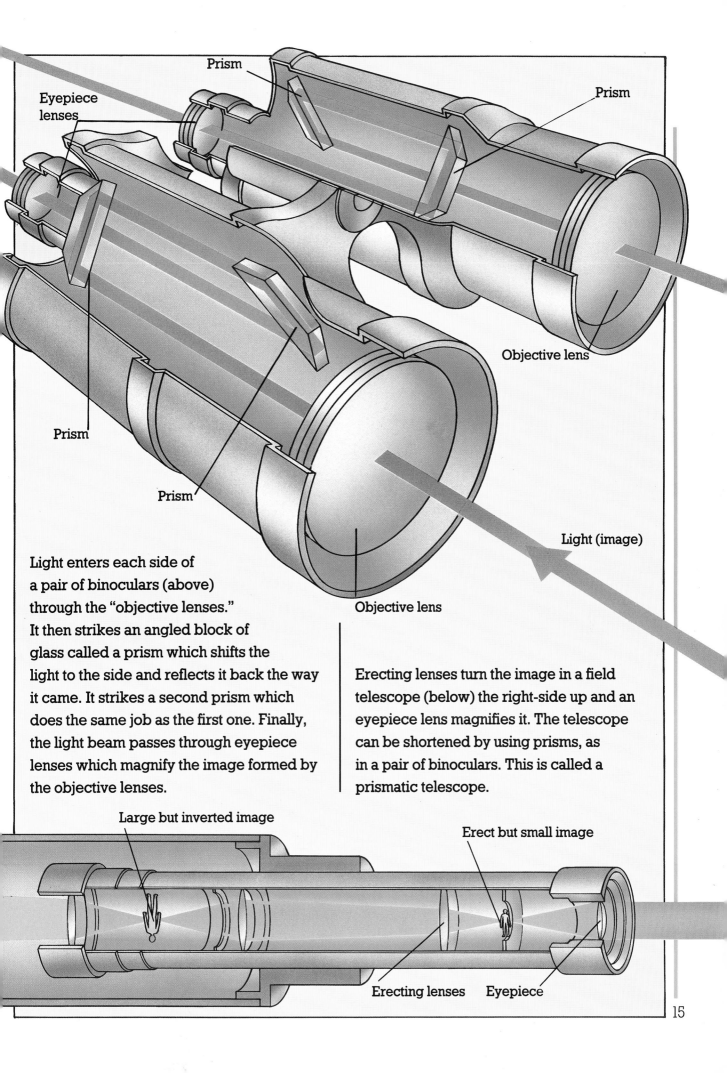

Prism

Eyepiece
lenses

Prism

Prism

Objective lens

Prism

Objective lens

Light (image)

Light enters each side of
a pair of binoculars (above)
through the "objective lenses."
It then strikes an angled block of
glass called a prism which shifts the
light to the side and reflects it back the way
it came. It strikes a second prism which
does the same job as the first one. Finally,
the light beam passes through eyepiece
lenses which magnify the image formed by
the objective lenses.

Erecting lenses turn the image in a field
telescope (below) the right-side up and an
eyepiece lens magnifies it. The telescope
can be shortened by using prisms, as
in a pair of binoculars. This is called a
prismatic telescope.

Large but inverted image

Erect but small image

Erecting lenses   Eyepiece

RADIATION AND ATMOSPHERE

Radiation is a type of energy that travels from its source, such as a star, in electromagnetic waves known as "rays." Different types of rays cross vast distances in space at the speed of light (168,000 miles a second).

When this radiation pierces the layers of hot and cold air that form our atmosphere, each type of ray is affected differently. For instance, some of the sun's rays are trapped by the layers of hot and cold air and others pass through to earth where we see and feel them as light and warmth. Another group of rays pass through, but they are invisible. These include radio, infrared, ultraviolet, gamma and X rays. All of these have wavelengths outside the spectrum of colors which mix to form white light.

These invisible rays are weakened or

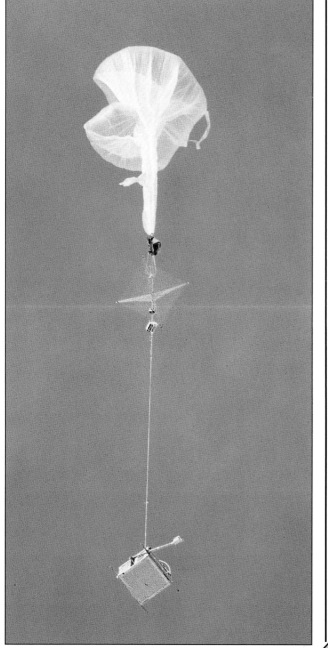

The photo left shows how a lighter-than-air balloon carries up a telescope.

X rays cannot be focused by the mirrors that are used in other telescopes. The X rays would travel through a normal mirror! However, they *can* be deflected when they strike a smooth surface at a very shallow angle. An X ray telescope is shown below. X rays entering the telescope (the opening is at the foot of page) skim across the slightly angled surface, the X ray optics, before they pass through the rest of the telescope and onto X ray detectors.

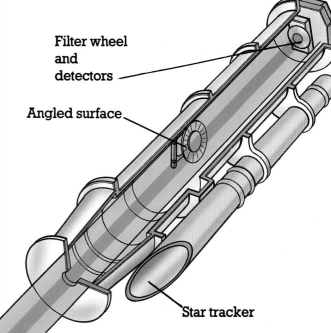

Filter wheel and detectors

Angled surface

Star tracker

distorted by the earth's atmosphere, but they can reveal secrets about objects in outer space, such as exploding stars, which are too faint to be seen with optical telescopes, or which give off only a little visible radiation. Scientists have developed special types of telescope that can detect these invisible types of radiation. The diagram (below) shows where these instruments work best.

The earth's atmosphere causes problems for most telescopes. Optical ones work best when sited on high mountains. As the atmosphere reflects or absorbs most of the radiation arriving here from the rest of the universe, Infrared (IR) telescopes need to be launched by rockets to orbit as satellites; and X ray telescopes are lifted aloft with the aid of large balloons. Radio telescopes, on the other hand, work very well at ground level.

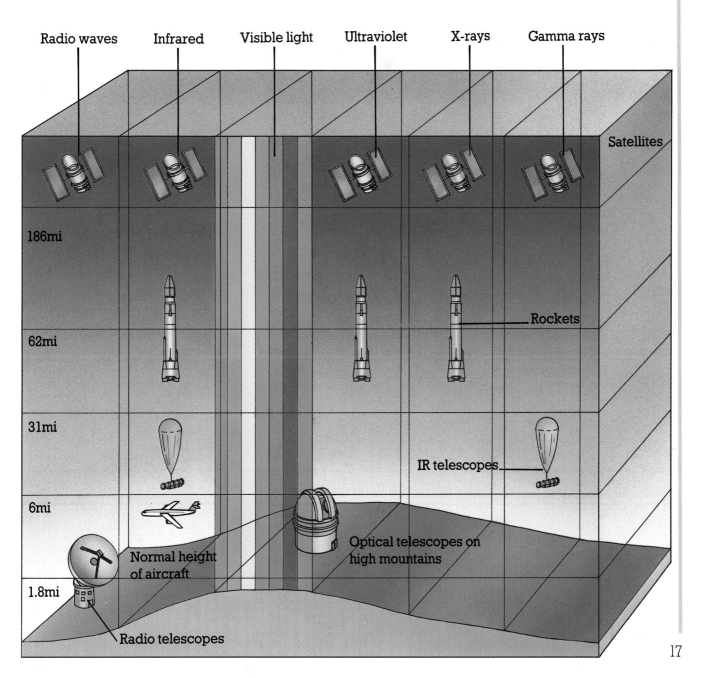

VIEWING THE SUN

No matter how much the stars are magnified by the most powerful telescopes, they are so incredibly far away that they never appear larger than points of light. The one exception to this in the entire universe is our own star, the sun. It contains 99.9 percent of the matter in the whole Solar System. Its force of gravity controls the movements of the nine planets, the asteroids, meteors and comets, and it provides the visible light and heat that sustains all life on earth.

Scientists study the sun to try to improve their understanding of its behavior and how it affects the earth and the other planets. An ordinary photograph of the sun reveals dark spots called sunspots and long fiery tongues stretching out into space from its atmosphere, the corona. They indicate magnetic disturbances. A special telescope, a coronograph, is used to study the corona.

The MacMath Solar Telescope at the Kitt Peak National Observatory in Arizona does not look like any other telescope. Only a tiny part of it is visible above ground. Sunlight strikes a mirror 5 feet across at the top. This mirror moves to keep the sun in view as the earth spins. The sunlight is reflected down to the end of a long tunnel, reflected back again and finally directed into the observing room. Here, an image of the sun measuring 33.5 inches in diameter can be projected onto a screen or studied by sensitive instruments. The instruments work at their best in the cool, even temperatures found deep underground, but there is an added cooling system.

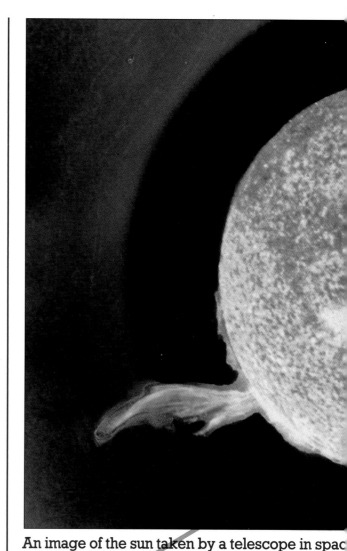

An image of the sun taken by a telescope in space

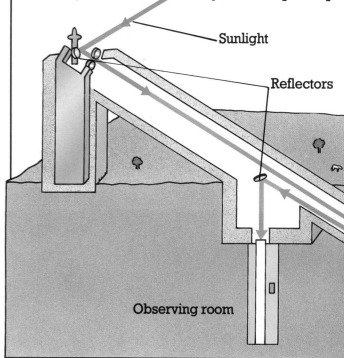

Sunlight

Reflectors

Observing room

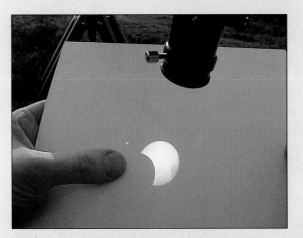

Sun

Projected image of solar eclipse

The image shows "sunspots" and a "flare."

Viewing sunspots and solar eclipses

Sunlight is so intense that looking directly at the sun can permanently damage the eyes. The only safe way to observe the sun is to use a telescope to project it onto white cardboard held underneath, with black cardboard surrounding the eyepiece. The observer should aim and focus the telescope by looking for the sun's image on the cardboard, *never* by looking through the telescope. Any sunspots on the sun's surface will appear as dark spots on the bright disk.

WARNING: NEVER LOOK DIRECTLY
AT THE SUN

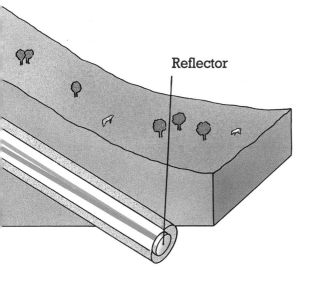

Reflector

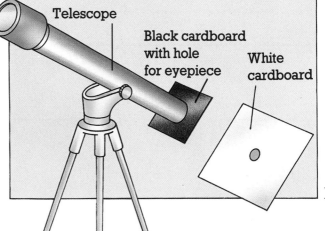

Telescope

Black cardboard
with hole
for eyepiece

White
cardboard

SIGNALS FROM SPACE

Many objects in space send out radio waves which can be detected on earth. The radio waves are produced when hot objects send out a wide range of wavelengths including radio waves, or when electrically charged particles called electrons travel through a magnetic field and their paths are bent into tight spirals.

By comparing images of the same star or galaxy taken in visible light with records or images of radio wavelengths, astronomers can learn much more about the chemical processes and energy changes going on inside it.

Radio astronomy does not only offer another way of studying known objects. It can discover objects that would otherwise not be found. The most distant objects in the universe are so dim that optical telescopes cannot detect them. Some of these are powerful radio sources. Radio telescopes record them as shining brightly from the edge of the universe and so provide information about the universe's incredible size.

Radio telescope in the Eifel hills, Germany, the largest steerable radio dish in the world.

The intense magnetic field of a dark, collapsed star called a neutron star shapes its radio emissions into two beams on opposite sides of the star. As the star spins rapidly, the beams sweep past the earth, to a radio telescope looking like the flashing of a lighthouse. These pulsing radio sources are known as pulsars. When they were discovered in 1967, it was at first thought that they might be radio signals sent by intelligent beings in other galaxies. It was soon discovered that this is not so.

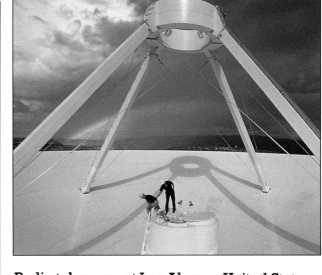

Radio telescope at Los Alamos, United States.

A radio telescope dish focuses radio waves onto a detector at the dish's focal point. In this respect it is like the mirror of a reflecting telescope. The detector produces an electrical signal that matches the strength of the radio waves. This can be shown on a screen or printed on paper. Today, the radio signals are processed by computer (see below) to give an image of the object that produced them. The computer can also add colors to the image to show up different intensities of radio energy more clearly.

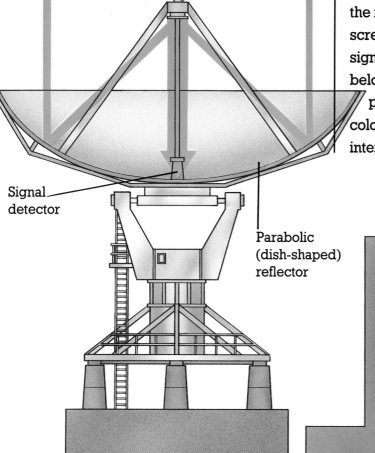

Focal point of aerial

Signal detector

Parabolic (dish-shaped) reflector

Electrical signal processing

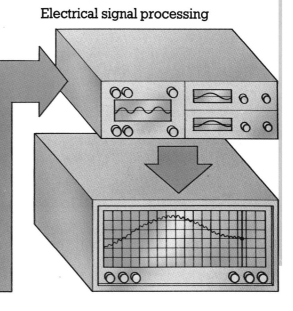

COLORED LIGHT

In a clear night sky each star appears to have a color. They are always either blue-white, white, yellow, orange or red. The red ones may look hotter to us but they are at about 5,432°F, while the blue-white stars are around 45,032°F.

The best way to study a star's light is with an instrument called a spectroscope attached to a telescope. This splits the star's light into a band of separate colors by passing it through a prism. Black lines appear in several places on the "rainbow"-like spectrum of colors. These are caused by the star's atmosphere absorbing certain wavelengths of light, and they show which chemicals are present in the star's outer layers.

Most stars are rushing away from the Earth at great speed, and the black lines in their light are shifted toward the red end of the spectrum. The size of this "red-shift" indicates how quickly each star is flying away. From this, astronomers know how quickly the universe is expanding. The red-shift of galaxies shows that the brightest galaxies in the sky range from about 170,000 to 50 million light years away.

Pictures can be made to reveal more information than is clear from an ordinary optical photograph (lower right). This is done by a process called computerized image enhancement. Different wavelengths of invisible radiation from space, such as radio or infrared, can be shown in "false" colors, as in a "radio map" photograph of a galaxy (top right). The brightest colors usually show where the most radiation at the chosen wavelength is being emitted.

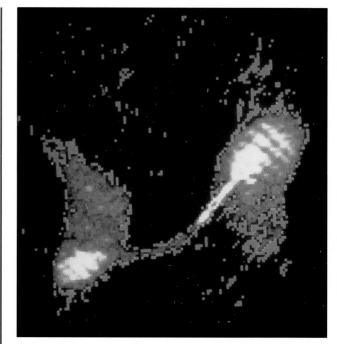

Image enhancement of galaxy NGC 326

Optical photograph of a spiral galaxy

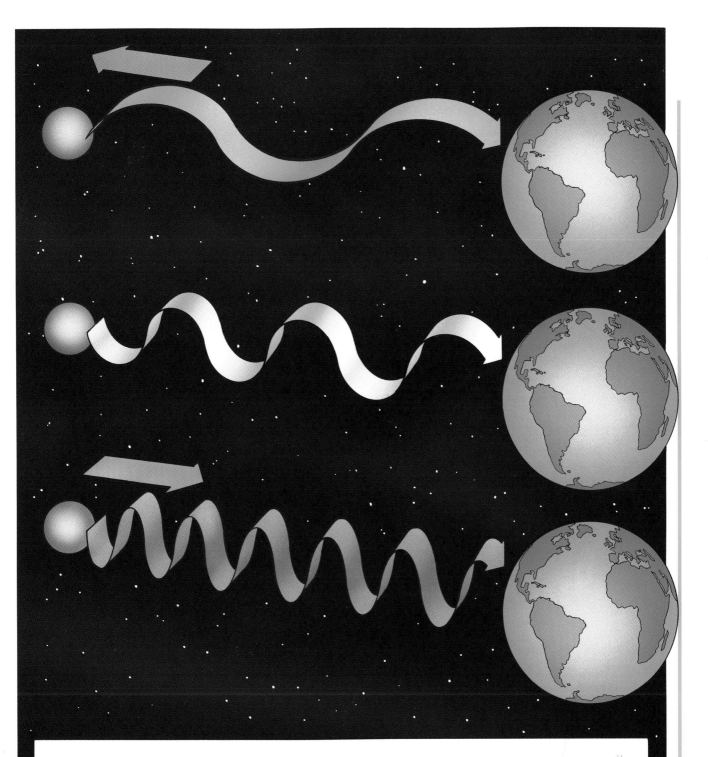

How colors show a star's movement

Astronomers can tell which way and how fast stars are moving in space by studying their light with an instrument called a spectroscope. This contains a prism which spreads the light into a rainbow-like band (a spectrum) with a pattern of thin black lines. When light waves coming from a star are of short wavelength, the black lines cluster near the color blue. This shows that the star is approaching us (bottom). If the star's light waves are long, the lines "shift" toward the red area of the spectrum. This shows that the star is moving away (top). When the lines are spread evenly and no shift occurs it means that there is no change in the distance between the star and earth (middle).

THE SPACE TELESCOPE

The Hubble Space Telescope (HST) is the largest space observatory ever built. The 43-feet-long 11-ton reflecting telescope was launched from the payload bay of the U.S. Space Shuttle in April 1990. It was designed to provide astronomers with images of objects such as galaxies that are up to 14,000 billion light years away at the edge of the universe or detailed pictures of the outer planets. From its position in orbit high above the earth's atmosphere, it can receive images that are ten times sharper than those picked up by any earth-based optical telescope.

While the HST was being tested in space, it was discovered that its main mirror, 8 ft across, had been made the wrong shape. The error was 2,000ths of a millimeter, but that was enough to make the telescope's images hazy. Fortunately, many of the telescope's components and systems were designed to be removed and replaced easily by astronauts. Although the faulty mirror cannot be replaced, a device that will correct the mirror's fault can be inserted. The images can also be improved by computer on earth.

The telescope was launched from the Space Shuttle Orbiter using its robot arm. When the Orbiter was safely in space, the payload bay doors were opened (1). Then the robot arm grasped the telescope and lifted it out of the payload bay (2). Finally, the telescope's solar panels were unrolled and its aperture door opened to begin testing the telescope's instruments (3). The Hubble Space Telescope will have a lifespan of 15 years.

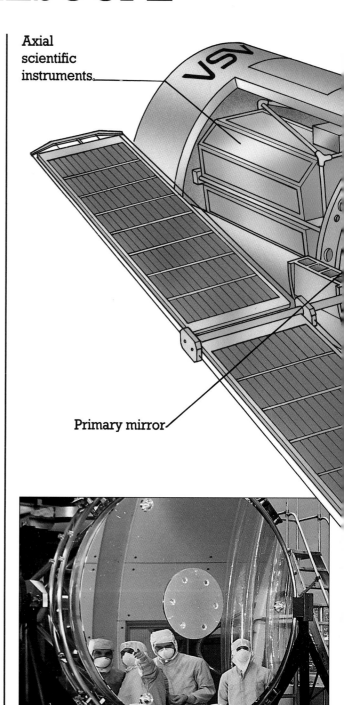

Axial scientific instruments.

Primary mirror

Inspecting the main mirror before fitting

1.

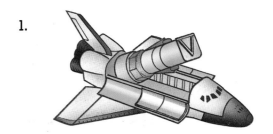

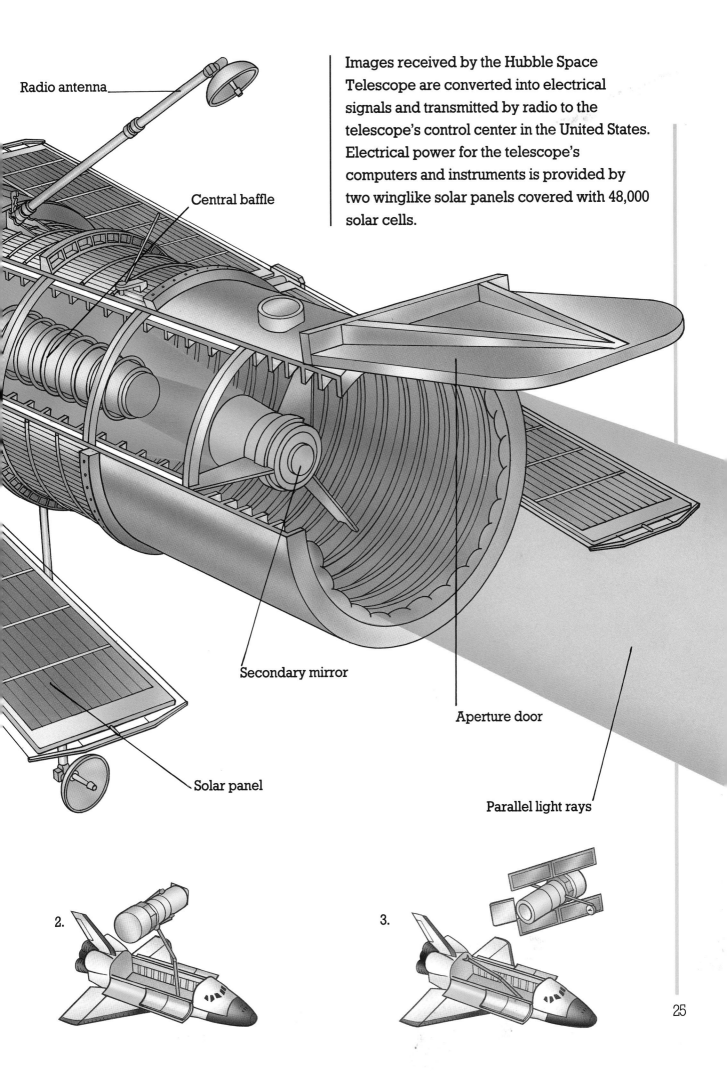

Radio antenna

Central baffle

Images received by the Hubble Space Telescope are converted into electrical signals and transmitted by radio to the telescope's control center in the United States. Electrical power for the telescope's computers and instruments is provided by two winglike solar panels covered with 48,000 solar cells.

Secondary mirror

Aperture door

Solar panel

Parallel light rays

2.

3.

25

SPECIAL TELESCOPES

Astronomers would like to build larger reflectors to gather more light and enable them to see faint objects more clearly. Large mirrors are distorted by changes in temperature and also by their own weight. One answer is to replace the large mirror with several smaller mirrors. The mirrors are controlled so that the image formed by each is directed to a central point, where they act together as one huge mirror.

Perhaps the strangest type of telescope is that which can only work deep underground. The photograph top-right shows part of one such "neutrino trap." This operates in a special chamber inside the Mont Blanc tunnel deep within the French Alps. Neutrinos are tiny particles produced by the nuclear fission in stars. Most of those that reach the earth come from the sun. Others have come to us from distant parts of the universe and have taken millions of years to get here.

The Multiple-Mirror Telescope (MMT) perches on top of Mount Hopkins in Arizona.

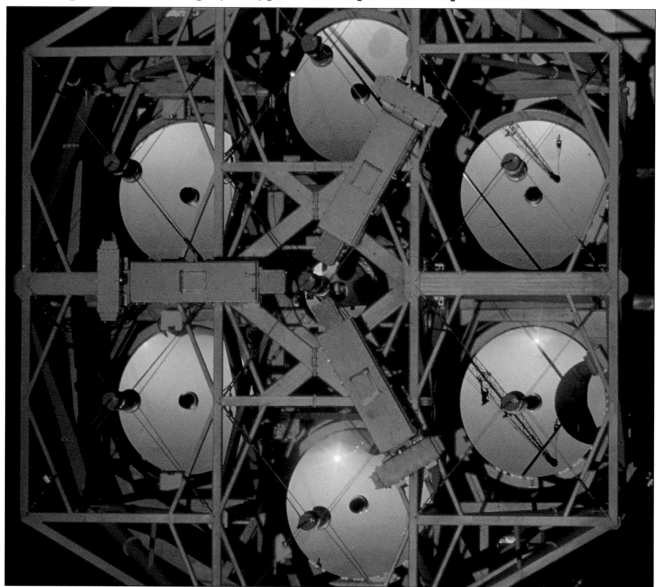

The light-sensitive equipment on an underground telescope.

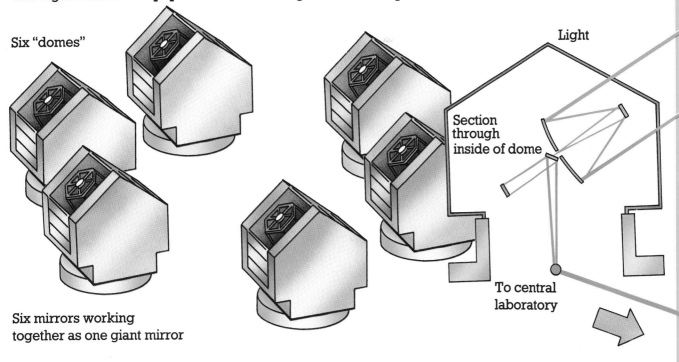

Six "domes"

Six mirrors working
together as one giant mirror

Light

Section
through
inside of dome

To central
laboratory

Neutrinos are even smaller than atoms, and they pass right through the earth. Other types of radiation make them very difficult to detect above ground. However, this neutrino trap is shielded by 19,685 feet of solid rock. It has metal tanks filled with a liquid similar to cleaning fluid. When a neutrino passes through these it emits a faint flash of light. Scientists studying these flashes say that some neutrinos have come from stars which no longer exist.

Each mirror in a multiple-mirror telescope is controlled independently so that the images formed by all the mirrors come together in a central laboratory. The Mount Hopkins Multiple-Mirror Telescope (left) consists of six mirrors, each 6 ft across, as good as a single mirror 15 ft across. Even larger multiple-mirror telescopes made from several dozen small mirrors arranged like the petals of a flower are being planned. They will be as good as reflectors of 33 ft across. Six together will act like a 82 ft-diameter mirror.

THE HISTORY OF TELESCOPES

The telescope is thought to have been invented in 1609 by a Dutch eyeglass-maker called Jan Lippershey. Within a year, news of Lippershey's invention reached the Italian astronomer, Galileo Galilei. Galileo soon made his own telescopes. They were tiny compared to today's giant instruments. The eyeglass lenses he used were at most 1 inch across. Even so, Galileo's telescopes enabled him to make a series of very important discoveries between 1610 and 1619. Some of his discoveries include craters and mountains on the moon, and moons orbiting the planet Jupiter.

Sir William Herschel 1731-1814.

Galileo, the earliest telescope-user.

The great English scientist, Sir Isaac Newton, tried to solve the refracting telescope's major problem. Its lenses split light into different colors which are focused at different points, blurring the image. Newton's solution was to use mirrors instead of lenses, because mirrors do not suffer from this color-smearing effect. Newton invented the reflecting telescope, or "reflector." He presented his invention to the Royal Society in London in 1671.

The German-born astronomer William Herschel built larger and larger reflectors. The biggest had a mirror 4 ft across. The third Earl of Rosse built an even bigger reflector in the 1840s. It had a 6 ft mirror. With it, Rosse was the first person to see the spiral shape of some galaxies.

In the 1930s Karl Jansky, working at the Bell Telephone Laboratories in the United States, discovered radio signals coming from the center of our galaxy. Astronomers were slow to realize its importance, but Jansky's discovery eventually developed into the modern science of radio astronomy with infra-red, X ray and radio telescopes.

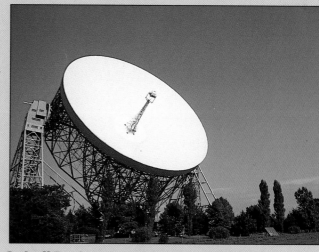

Jodrell Bank radio telescope, England.

The late 19th century and early 20th century was a very active period of telescope building. A refractor with a 3 ft-wide objective lens, built by Alvan Clark and George Hale, in 1897 near Chicago, is still the world's biggest refractor. Hale also built a reflector with a mirror 16 ft across at Mount Palomar in 1948.

Most telescopes built in recent years have been smaller, with mirrors of about 13 ft across. New electronic light detectors and computerized image processing enable these telescopes to outperform the larger ones. With modern communication links, astronomers operate telescopes at a distance.

A modern reflector on an island in Hawaii.

Astronomers are building large reflectors again. Mirrors more than about 26 ft across are distorted by their own weight. Reflectors in the 1990s will be bigger than this, up to 52 ft across, by linking together several small, individually steered mirrors. As most of the radiation from the universe is blocked or distorted by the earth's atmosphere, telescopes are increasingly placed in space where they can "see" further, with more clarity and detail.

Facts and figures

The most powerful optical telescope in the world is also the world's largest reflector. The telescope, on Mount Semirodriki in the Soviet Union, has a 20 ft mirror weighing 70 tons. It is so powerful that it could detect the light from a candle 15,000 mi away.

The largest refractor ever built was a 4 ft horizontal telescope built for the Paris Exposition in 1900. However, the instrument was so cumbersome that it was dismantled after the Exposition.

The largest successful refractor in the world is the 1.01m (40-inch) telescope built at the Yerkes Observatory near Chicago. Its lens weighs a quarter of a ton.

The largest radio telescope was built in a natural hollow in the earth, in Arecibo on the island of Puerto Rico. The dish, which measures 1,000 ft across, was built in 1963 and rebuilt in 1974 to improve its performance.

The first astronomical observatories in space were the U.S. Orbiting Solar Observatory satellites. They began to be launched in 1962. Since then, numerous American-, Soviet- and European-built telescope-carrying satellites have been put in orbit.

The largest telescope in space is the Hubble Space Telescope. The tube of this optical telescope measures 43 ft long by 14 ft in diameter. The whole craft weighs 11 tons.

GLOSSARY

comet
Lumps of ice, dust and rock in orbit around the sun. Some comets, such as Halley's, are at times visible from earth.

constellation
A group of stars. In the past, constellations were named after animals or figures from legend that their patterns appeared to resemble, for example The Great Bear, The Plough, Taurus the Bull, Cancer the Crab. In reality, the stars were not close to each other at all. The whole sky is now divided into 88 areas named after the old constellations.

coronagraph
A telescope for observing the sun's corona, the outermost region of its atmosphere where there is intense burning of gases. A metal disk the size of the sun's normal image is placed inside the tube so that it allows only the light from the corona to pass around it to the rest of the instrument for projecting on to a screen. (The sun should never be viewed directly.)

electromagnetic radiation
Energy waves consisting of electric and magnetic fields at right angles to each other traveling through space. The radiation type (light, radio, X rays, etc) depends on the wavelength of the waves. All electromagnetic radiation travels at 984 million feet per second.

focal point
The point where parallel light rays bent by a mirror or a lens meet.

gamma rays
Electromagnetic radiation with wavelengths shorter than X rays.

infrared
Electromagnetic radiation beyond the red end of the visible light spectrum.

light
Electromagnetic radiation with wavelengths from 0.4 to 0.77 millionths of a meter. The human eye is sensitive to this narrow band of radiation only.

light year
The distance light travels in space in one year – 5,878,000,000,000 miles – which astronomers use as a measure of the great distances in the universe.

parabola
The shape of an optical telescope main mirror and radio telescope dish. It focuses radiation from space on a point in front of the mirror or dish.

photomultiplier
A device used on professional astronomers' optical telescopes used to make a faint light much brighter. The light strikes a metal plate and knocks particles called electrons out of it. They strike a second plate and knock more electrons out of that and so on. The large electric current produced is then used to form an image on a television screen.

primary mirror
The main mirror of a reflecting telescope, or reflector.

prism

A triangular block of glass or transparent plastic used in optical instruments to split light into its different wavelengths or colors, to turn an image upside down, or to reflect light back the way it came.

radiation

Energy in the form of a range, or spectrum, of electrical and magnetic (electromagnetic) waves, including light, radio, X rays, ultraviolet and infrared. Astronomical telescopes detect radiation from space.

secondary mirror

A small mirror used to reflect the light from a telescope's primary mirror to the telescope's eyepiece or viewing point.

seeing disk

The size of the blurred image of a point source of light seen through a telescope pointed at the sky. The smaller the seeing disk is, the finer is the detail that the telescope can show in its images.

ultraviolet

Electromagnetic radiation with wavelengths shorter than violet light, ranging from a ten millionth to a thousand millionth of a meter.

X rays

Electromagnetic radiation with shorter wavelengths than ultraviolet radiation, ranging from a thousand millionth of a meter down to a billionth of a meter.

Our galaxy, the "Milky Way"

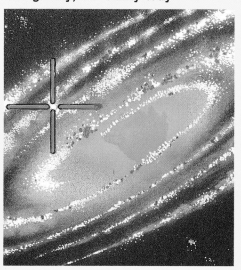

Our sun within the "Milky Way"

Our Solar System seen from space

INDEX

Photographic credits
Cover and pages 6, 7 top left and top right, 9, 12, 16, 19, 20, 21, 22 top, 24, 26, 27, 28 bottom and 29: Science Photo Library; pages 7 bottom left, 13 and 14: Spectrum Colour Library; page 7 bottom right: Frank Spooner Pictures; pages 18-19 and 22 bottom: Zefa Picture Library; page 28 top and middle: Popperfoto.